Thank you to my mother and father, for all the countless memories of traveling to dog shows, of winning and losing, and learning lifelong lessons. Thank you to all my faithful friends, and loyal companions, which offered me unconditional love throughout my life.
--Cheryl Schreiner

Text Copyright © 2015 Cheryl Schreiner
Illustrations Copyright © 2015 Cynthia Pierson

All rights reserved. No part of the book may be reproduced in any manner without the expressed written consent of the copyright owners, except in the case of brief excerpts in critical reviews and artices. All inquiries should be addressed to:

Island Media Publishing, LLC
120 N. 15th St.
Fernandina Beach, FL 32034
www.islandmediapublishing.com

ISBN 978-0-9829908-3-4
Library of Congress 2015955794

Island Media Publishing, LLC

These are paw prints.
They are not just paw prints of any dog, they are pawprints of a very famous show dog named Jack.

Jack has traveled throughout the world. He has appeared on TV. Jack is famous.

Many people have seen Jack and heard of his fame. However, Jack was not always famous. It took a lot of hard work and practice.

Jack is a show dog. A show dog must be kept very clean and tidy.

A show dog must be bathed and brushed.

A show dog must be walked and exercised in a very special way.

Jack was always clean and tidy, bathed and brushed, and always had just the right amount of exercise.

Jack was just right. So he went into the dog show ring looking his best.

All the hard work and practice paid off for Jack, and he won first place at the dog show.

Jack was very happy!

Jack was a champion show dog.